TRUTH AND GRACE MEMORY BOOK

BOOK 1

AGE 2 – 4TH GRADE

THOMAS K ASCOL, EDITOR

Published by

Founders Press

Committed to historic Baptist principles
P.O. Box 150931 • Cape Coral, FL 33915
Phone (239) 772-1400 • Fax: (239) 772-1140
Electronic Mail: founders@founders.org or
Website: http://www.founders.org
©2000 Founders Press
Reprinted 2005

Printed in the United States of America

ISBN: 0-9705248-0-3

Unless otherwise indicated, Scripture quotations in this publication are from the New King James Version of the Bible ©1979, 1980, 1984, 1988 Thomas Nelson, Inc., Nashville, TN.

A Catechism for Boys and Girls is reprinted with adaptation with permission from Carey Publications Ltd., 75 Woodhill Road, Leeds LS16 7BZ, United Kingdom.

Cover Art by Jonathan Reisinger
Cover Design by Kenneth Puls

Introduction

Dr. Thomas K. Ascol

A Word to Parents

The Bible teaches that children are "a heritage from the Lord" and that "the fruit of the womb is His reward" (Psalm 127:3). Each child is a gift from God. This makes you, as a parent, God's steward. He has entrusted you with one (or more) of His greatest blessings. He has given to you one of His highest callings.

In our day the challenge of parenting has never been greater. Too many moms and dads give in to the temptation to merely "get by." Simply making it through with the fewest possible conflicts becomes the goal. When this attitude is adopted, parents become passive and children learn to be manipulative. One of the saddest, most tragic sights ever to be observed in the Christian Church is a home where parents have defaulted on the responsibilities that God has entrusted to them.

Children are not designed to raise themselves. That is why God gives them parents. Christian parents have been given the specific, gracious duty of raising their children "in the training and admonition of the Lord" (Ephesians 6:4). You cannot be passive and fulfill this responsibility to "bring them up" in the proper way. Prayer, discipline, Godly example, and consistent, continuous, clear instruction are the tools that we must employ.

The responsibility to teach children foundational, eternal, life-changing truth from God's Word is laid squarely upon the shoulders of parents by the Lord Himself. Consider the charge that He has given to moms and dads:

> Hear, O Israel: The LORD our God, the LORD is one! You shall love the LORD your God with all your heart,

with all your soul, and with all your strength. And these words which I command you today shall be in your heart. You shall teach them diligently to your children, and shall talk of them when you sit in your house, when you walk by the way, when you lie down, and when you rise up (Deuteronomy 6:4–7).

The primary responsibility for teaching your children about God does not belong to the Sunday School or the pastor or any program in the church. God has entrusted this important work to you, dear parent. If you do not invest your time and effort to teach your children about God, be assured that someone else will. The television and theater will teach them that God, if He exists at all, is an irrelevant, indulgent being that is little more than a nice, kindly old man. If you do not teach your children truth and righteousness, be assured that there are a multitude of teachers in this world who would deceive them into thinking that "truth" and morality are relative ideas that can be shaped to fit anyone's beliefs or standards.

Your church stands with you against the false teachers of our age which would destroy the souls of our young people. You have every right to expect that sermons and Sunday School lessons will reinforce the godly principles which you are trying to teach at home. But you have no right to expect the church to take the place of the home. God has given to *parents* the responsibility of teaching their children divine truth.

The *Truth & Grace Memory Book* (TAG) has been designed to help you fulfill this assignment. The emphasis, obviously, is on memorization. Some modern educators have questioned the wisdom of teaching young children to memorize. Concern usually centers on the fear that the child is merely committing to memory meaningless words. This is a real danger—that we will be satisfied with hearing our children merely recite back to us words and sentences about which they have no real understanding. That is why parents must *teach* their children the material in TAG. Personal understanding should always be the goal of our teaching. But understanding will grow (mine has; hasn't yours?). Truth committed to the memory provides the building blocks for such growth.

Discuss the material being memorized with your child. This should be done during the actual memorization as well as at other opportune times in the day. Daily experiences and observations provide a world of opportunities to *illustrate* and **apply** God's Word. For example, the inevitable "night frights" which young children occasionally have, become wonderful occasions to comfortingly remind them that, though we cannot see God, He always sees us. Take time to *define* difficult terms. *Question* your child in order to discover the level of his understanding. When you feel that understanding is being achieved, *pray* with and for the child, including in your prayer some of the concepts just discussed. *Expect* your child to learn, and rejoice with him over his growth in knowledge and understanding of God's Word.

No matter what the age of your child, if you will begin immediately, and continue consistently, to teach them with TAG, you will instill in them a comprehensive awareness of the Bible's whole system of revealed truth. Obviously, the earlier a child begins, the better. But TAG has been designed to be useful to young people as well as to children and preschoolers.

Three primary ingredients make TAG a valuable tool in teaching our children God's revealed truth. First and foremost is the Word of God. Several passages have been carefully selected for memorization. Key Bible verses as well as longer portions are designed to introduce children to the overall scope and purpose of God's creative, providential and redemptive activity. The student who completes TAG will read (among other things) the New Testament twice, the 4 Gospels three times, Proverbs five times and the book of Psalms twice. He will memorize (among other texts) the Ten Commandments, the Beatitudes, the Lord's Prayer, 1 Corinthians 13, various psalms (including 119!), plus all the books of the Bible.

Why place such an emphasis on memorizing Scripture? Listen to the Psalmist's answer: "Your word I have hidden in my heart, that I might not sin against You!" (Psalm 119:11). Furthermore, consider the great promise God makes in Isaiah 55:10–11:

> For as the rain comes down, and the snow from heaven,
> and do not return there, but water the earth, and make it

bring forth and bud, that it may give seed to the sower and bread to the eater, so shall My word be that goes forth from My mouth; It shall not return to Me void, but it shall accomplish what I please, and it shall prosper in the thing for which I sent it.

God's Spirit uses the Scripture to speak to adults and children of all ages, calling them to faith in Christ and directing them in the paths of real discipleship. Therefore, as a parent who prays for the salvation and spiritual growth of your child, you must be diligent in teaching him or her the Word of God.

A second element in TAG is a selection of Christian hymns which are to be learned and memorized. Many of these are familiar (such as the Doxology) and can be learned by very small children. Others are not so well-known but are profound in their communication of biblical truth. In all, more than two dozen great hymns of the faith are included.

A third ingredient consists of three different Baptist catechisms, which are spread throughout the three books. The phrase "Baptist catechism" may sound strange to many contemporary Baptists. Some may even consider it to be a contradiction of terms. The truth of the matter, however, is that "catechism" is not a Roman Catholic or Lutheran or Presbyterian word. Rather, it is the anglicized version of the Greek word, *katekeo*, which simply means "to instruct." It appears, in various forms, several times in the Greek New Testament (it is translated as "instructed" in Luke 1:4 and Acts 18:25).

Obviously, then, anyone who has been instructed has in some sense been "catechized." But the word came to refer to a specific type of instruction early in church history. In the early church new Christians were taught the essentials of the faith by learning how to answer specific questions. Certain catechetical questions were grouped together and came to be referred to simply as a "catechism."

From the beginning modern-day Baptists (who emerged in the early 17th century) have employed various catechisms. Catechetical instruction was regarded as a valuable method of teaching both children and adults the doctrinal content of the Bible. Keach's Catechism (whose author, Benjamin Keach—a 17th-century English

Baptist—modeled it after *The Shorter Catechism of the Westminster Assembly*) was widely used among Baptists in both England and America. Charles Spurgeon (19th-century English Baptist leader) revised it slightly and reissued it for use in the Metropolitan Tabernacle. A modern version of this same catechism (*The Shorter Catechism: A Baptist Version*) is introduced in Book 2. A simpler one (*A Catechism for Boys and Girls*) is introduced in Book 1. Tragically, the best known Protestant catechism in the world is largely unknown to most contemporary Baptists. The *Heidelberg Catechism* has been warmly received and widely used since its first German publication in 1563. A 17th-century English Baptist pastor, Hercules Collins, modified this catechism for his congregation and called it the *Orthodox Catechism*. Included in Book 3 is the *Heidelberg Catechism: A Baptist Version*.

Southern Baptists of an earlier day freely employed catechisms. One of the first publications which the Sunday School Board produced was a catechism by James Boyce, founder and first President of The Southern Baptist Theological Seminary. John Broadus also wrote a catechism which was published by the board in the 19th century. Lottie Moon used a catechism in her missionary work in China. It is only in recent generations that Southern Baptists have moved away from catechetical instruction as an important tool in teaching God's Word.

By learning a whole, well-constructed catechism a child (or adult for that matter) will be introduced to the overall biblical scheme of salvation. Such discipline will frame the mind for receiving and understanding every part of the Bible. A good catechism helps one to read the Bible theologically.

For these reasons, catechism questions are utilized in TAG. Combined with the other elements, catechetical instruction can prove to be a powerful tool in training our children to be strong in the Lord.

Much hard work has gone into the production of these memory books. Karen Leach and Judy Veilleux have spent long hours in deliberation and refinement in order to see this project completed. We have borrowed ideas from earlier, similar efforts that have been utilized in other churches. Specifically, we built upon an earlier workbook by Paul Settle which was edited for Baptists by Fred Malone and further adapted by Bill Ascol. Rather than further adapt their work, we opted to redesign the idea and come up with a memory book that would more adequately meet the needs of the families of Grace Baptist Church. Now through Founders Press, these TAG books are being made available for wider use. It is with much hope and prayer that homes will be strengthened, children converted and established in the faith, and parents encouraged that this training guide has been produced. May God use it to gain much praise and glory for Himself through our church.

How to Use the Truth and Grace Memory Book

1. Make this memory book something very special in your child's life. Emphasize the importance of learning God's Word. If you are genuinely excited about it, most likely your children will be also.

2. Incorporate it into your regular time of family prayer and devotion. After you have read a portion of God's Word, or some Bible story book, and have prayed, take a few minutes to work on a specific verse or question. Learn to sing the hymns together as a family (You can do it! You simply have to make the effort.).

3. Encourage precise memorization. If they are going to spend the time and effort to learn it, they might as well learn it accurately.

4. Be very positive. Try not to let the memory book become a battleground where a contest of the wills (child's vs. parent's) occurs. This *does not* mean that you let the child dictate when he will or will not work on the material. Rather, do not let yourself get into the position where you are violating biblical principles (by employing rage, sarcasm, ridicule, empty threats, etc.) in your zeal to have your child learn the Bible!

5. Date each step. Throughout TAG there are places for the parent to signify that the student has completed the assignment. Treat each one as a significant milestone and encourage your child to keep progressing.

6. Go at your child's own rate. Children, like adults, learn differently and at different tempos. TAG is designed so that the material can be covered as quickly or slowly as needed. Do not hesitate to move beyond the stated age levels. Remember, these are merely suggestions.

7. Discuss the content of the verses, catechism questions or hymns being learned. Help your child understand what they are saying. Remember, the goal is spiritual understanding, *not* mechanical regurgitation.

8. Review. Avoid placing such an emphasis on advancement that your child is tempted to utilize only his or her short-term rather than long-term memory.

9. Rejoice. Your child is learning Bible truths that some adults will never know. Thank the Lord for the privilege of teaching your children about Him. Be encouraged as you hear them reciting the Word of God and expressing important biblical truths.

10. Pray. Ask God to drive His Word deep into the heart and conscience of each child. Pray that He will send His Spirit to teach them inwardly the truth about sin and judgment, heaven and hell, Jesus and salvation. As you diligently teach your children, labor in prayer for them until you see Christ being formed in them.

11. Encourage other parents. We all need it. Make a conscious effort to give it. Training our children in the way of the Lord is a high calling. We are constantly tempted to neglect it. We all fail at some point and at some time. Resolve to be an encourager.

OUTLINE

The following is an outline of memory work from Book 1 divided into suggested age/grade levels. If you are not beginning age 2 or 3, we suggest that you begin with the appropriate scripture, hymns, etc. for your child, as well as with question #1 of *A Catechism for Boys and Girls*. The catechism is written in a systematic format with each question built upon those before it. The memorization of the whole catechism will expose the child to a solid doctrinal foundation.

Ages 2 and 3

Age 4

Age 5 (Kindergarten)

1st Grade

2nd Grade

Ages 2 and 3

Genesis 1:1
In the beginning God created the heavens and the earth.

Date: _____

Matthew 22:37
Jesus said to him, *"You shall love the LORD your God with all your heart, with all your soul, and with all your mind."*

Date: _____

John 3:16
For God so loved the world that He gave His only begotten Son, that whoever believes in Him should not perish but have everlasting life.

Date: _____

Matthew 22:39
And the second is like it: *"You shall love your neighbor as yourself."*

Date: _____

John 14:6
Jesus said to him, "I am the way, the truth, and the life. No one comes to the Father except through Me."

Date: _____

Luke 19:10
For the Son of Man has come to seek and to save that which was lost.

Date: _____

Ephesians 6:1

Children, obey your parents in the Lord, for this is right.

Date: _____

John 1:1

In the beginning was the Word, and the Word was with God, and the Word was God.

Date: _____

Hymn: *Jesus Loves Me* (Verse 1)

Jesus loves me! this I know,
For the Bible tells me so;
Little ones to Him belong;
They are weak, but He is strong.

Refrain:
Yes, Jesus loves me!
Yes, Jesus loves me!
Yes, Jesus loves me!
The Bible tells me so.

Date: _____

Hymn: *Doxology*

Praise God, from Whom all blessings flow;
Praise Him, all creatures here below;
Praise Him above, ye heavenly host;
Praise Father, Son, and Holy Ghost.

Amen.

Date: _____

Mid-Year Review by Teacher: _____
Year-End Review by Teacher: _____

Age 4

Psalm 122:1

I was glad when they said to me,
"Let us go into the house of the LORD."

Date: _____

John 4:24

God is Spirit, and those who worship Him must worship in spirit and truth.

Date: _____

Matthew 6:9–13 (The Lord's Prayer)

In this manner, therefore, pray:
Our Father in heaven,
Hallowed be Your name.
Your kingdom come.
Your will be done
On earth as it is in heaven.
Give us this day our daily bread.
And forgive us our debts,
As we forgive our debtors.
And do not lead us into temptation,
But deliver us from the evil one.
For Yours is the kingdom and the power and the glory forever.
Amen.

Date: _____

Proverbs 1:8

My son, hear the instruction of your father,
And do not forsake the law of your mother;

Date: _____

John 1:1,14

In the beginning was the Word, and the Word was with God, and the Word was God. And the Word became flesh and dwelt among us, and we beheld His glory, the glory as of the only begotten of the Father, full of grace and truth.

Date: _____

Proverbs 4:1

Hear, my children, the instruction of a father,
And give attention to know understanding.

Date: _____

Psalm 103:1

Bless the LORD, O my soul;
And all that is within me, bless His holy name!

Date: _____

Isaiah 6:3

And one cried to another and said:
"Holy, holy, holy is the LORD of hosts;
The whole earth is full of His glory!"

Date: _____

Psalm 145:3

Great is the LORD, and greatly to be praised;
And His greatness is unsearchable.

Date: _____

Psalm 145:8

The LORD is gracious and full of compassion,
Slow in anger and great in mercy.

Date: _____

Hymn: *Jesus Loves Me* (all verses)

> Jesus loves me! this I know,
> For the Bible tells me so;
> Little ones to Him belong;
> They are weak, but He is strong.

>> Refrain:
>>> Yes, Jesus loves me!
>>> Yes, Jesus loves me!
>>> Yes, Jesus loves me!
>>> The Bible tells me so.

> Jesus loves me! He who died
> Heaven's gate to open wide;
> He will wash away my sin,
> Let His little child come in.

>> (Refrain)

> Jesus loves me! loves me still,
> Tho' I'm very weak and ill;
> From His shining throne on high,
> Comes to watch me where I lie.

>> (Refrain)

> Jesus loves me! He will stay
> Close beside me all the way;
> Thou hast bled and died for me,
> I will henceforth live for Thee.

>> (Refrain)

Date: _____

Age 4

Hymn: *Holy, Holy, Holy* (verse 1)

Holy, holy, holy! Lord God Almighty!
Early in the morning our song shall rise to Thee;
Holy, holy, holy, merciful and mighty!
God in three Persons, blessed Trinity!

Amen.

Date: _____

Mid-Year Review by Teacher: _____
Year-End Review by Teacher: _____

Age 5
(Kindergarten)

Psalm 23

The LORD is my shepherd;
I shall not want.
He makes me to lie down in green pastures;
He leads me beside the still waters.
He restores my soul;
He leads me in the paths of righteousness
For His name's sake.

Yea, though I walk through the valley of the shadow of death,
I will fear no evil;
For You are with me;
Your rod and Your staff, they comfort me.

You prepare a table before me in the presence of my enemies;
You anoint my head with oil;
My cup runs over.
Surely goodness and mercy shall follow me
All the days of my life;
And I will dwell in the house of the LORD
Forever.

Date: _____

Romans 6:23

For the wages of sin is death, but the gift of God is eternal life in
Christ Jesus our Lord.

Date: _____

John 6:35

And Jesus said to them, "I am the bread of life. He who comes to Me shall never hunger, and he who believes in Me shall never thirst."

Date: _____

Deuteronomy 6:4–5

"Hear, O Israel: The LORD our God, the LORD is one! You shall love the LORD your God with all your heart, with all your soul, and with all your strength."

Date: _____

John 1:29

The next day John saw Jesus coming toward him, and said, "Behold! The Lamb of God who takes away the sin of the world!"

Date: _____

Proverbs 4:1–2

Hear, my children, the instruction of a father,
And give attention to know understanding;
For I give you good doctrine:
Do not forsake my law.

Date: _____

Proverbs 1:8–9

My son, hear the instruction of your father,
And do not forsake the law of your mother;
For they will be a graceful ornament on your head,
And chains about your neck.

Date: _____

Psalm 145:8–9

The LORD is gracious and full of compassion,
Slow to anger and great in mercy.
The LORD is good to all,
And His tender mercies are over all His works.

Date: _____

Acts 16:31

So they said, "Believe on the Lord Jesus Christ, and you will be saved, you and your household."

Date: _____

Hymn: *Tell Me the Story of Jesus*

Tell me the story of Jesus,
Write on my heart every word;
Tell me the story most precious,
Sweetest that ever was heard.
Tell how the angels, in chorus,
Sang as they welcomed His birth,
"Glory to God in the highest!
Peace and good tidings to earth."

Refrain:
Tell me the story of Jesus,
Write on my heart every word;
Tell me the story most precious,
Sweetest that ever was heard.

Fasting alone in the desert,
Tell of the days that are past,
How for our sins He was tempted,
Yet was triumphant at last.

Tell of the years of His labor,
Tell of the sorrow He bore.
He was despised and afflicted,
Homeless, rejected and poor.

(Refrain)

Tell of the cross where they nailed Him,
Writhing in anguish and pain;
Tell of the grave where they laid Him,
Tell how He liveth again.
Love in that story so tender,
Clearer than ever I see.
Stay, let me weep while you whisper,
Love paid the ransom for me.

(Refrain)

Date: _____

Hymn: *Rejoice, the Lord is King* (verse 1)
Rejoice, the Lord is King!
Your Lord and King adore!
Rejoice, give thanks and sing,
And triumph evermore:
Lift up your heart, lift up your voice!
Rejoice, again I say, rejoice!

Amen.

Date: _____

Hymn: *Holy, Holy, Holy* (all verses)

Holy, holy, holy! Lord God Almighty!
Early in the morning our song shall rise to Thee;
Holy, holy, holy, merciful and mighty!
God in three Persons, blessed Trinity!

Holy, holy, holy! all the saints adore Thee,
Casting down their golden crowns around the glassy sea;
Cherubim and seraphim falling down before Thee,
Who wert, and art, and evermore shall be.

Holy, holy, holy! tho' the darkness hide Thee,
Tho' the eye of sinful man Thy glory may not see;
Only Thou art holy; there is none beside Thee,
Perfect in power, in love, and purity.

Holy, holy, holy! Lord God Almighty!
All Thy works shall praise Thy Name, in earth, and sky, and sea;
Holy, holy, holy; merciful and mighty!
God in three Persons, blessed Trinity!

Date: _____

Mid-Year Review by Teacher: _____
Year-End Review by Teacher: _____

Age 5 (Kindergarten)

1st Grade

Luke 2:8–15 (The story of Christ's birth)

Now there were in the same country shepherds living out in the fields, keeping watch over their flock by night. And behold, an angel of the Lord stood before them, and the glory of the Lord shone around them, and they were greatly afraid. Then the angel said to them, "Do not be afraid, for behold, I bring you good tidings of great joy which will be to all people. For there is born to you this day in the city of David a Savior, who is Christ the Lord. And this will be the sign to you: You will find a Babe wrapped in swaddling cloths, lying in a manger." And suddenly there was with the angel a multitude of the heavenly host praising God and saying:

"Glory to God in the highest,
And on earth peace, goodwill toward men!"

So it was, when the angels had gone away from them into heaven, that the shepherds said to one another, "Let us now go to Bethlehem and see this thing that has come to pass, which the Lord has made known to us."

Date: _____

John 11:25–26

Jesus said to her, "I am the resurrection and the life. He who believes in Me, though he may die, he shall live. And whoever lives and believes in Me shall never die. Do you believe this?"

Date: _____

Romans 10:9–10

If you confess with your mouth the Lord Jesus and believe in your heart that God has raised Him from the dead, you will be saved. For with the heart one believes unto righteousness, and with the mouth confession is made unto salvation.

Date: _____

Romans 6:23

For the wages of sin is death, but the gift of God is eternal life in Christ Jesus our Lord.

Date: _____

Romans 1:18

For the wrath of God is revealed from heaven against all ungodliness and unrighteousness of men, who suppress the truth in unrighteousness . . .

Date: _____

Romans 3:23

For all have sinned and fall short of the glory of God.

Date: _____

Psalm 8

O LORD, our Lord,
How excellent is Your name in all the earth,
Who have set Your glory above the heavens!

Out of the mouth of babes and nursing infants
You have ordained strength,
Because of Your enemies,
That You may silence the enemy and the avenger.
When I consider Your heavens, the work of Your fingers,
The moon and the stars, which You have ordained,
What is man that You are mindful of him,
And the son of man that You visit him?
For You have made him a little lower than the angels,
And You have crowned him with glory and honor.
You have made him to have dominion over the works of Your
    hands;
You have put all things under his feet,
All sheep and oxen—
Even the beasts of the field,
The birds of the air,
And the fish of the sea
That pass through the paths of the seas.

O LORD, our Lord,
How excellent is Your name in all the earth!

Date: _____

The Ten Commandments (summarized version)

1. You shall have no other gods before me.
2. You shall not make for yourself any carved image.
3. You shall not take the name of the LORD your God in vain.
4. Remember the Sabbath day, to keep it holy.
5. Honor your father and mother.
6. You shall not murder.
7. You shall not commit adultery.
8. You shall not steal.
9. You shall not bear false witness.
10. You shall not covet.

Date: _____

Hymn: *Fairest Lord Jesus*

Fairest Lord Jesus, Ruler of all nature,
O Thou of God and man the Son;
Thee will I cherish, Thee will I honor,
Thou, my soul's glory, joy and crown.

Fair are the meadows, Fairer still the woodlands,
Robed in the blooming garb of spring;
Jesus is fairer, Jesus is purer,
Who makes the woeful heart to sing.

Fair is the sunshine, Fairer still the moonlight,
And all the twinkling, starry host;
Jesus shines brighter, Jesus shines purer
Than all the angels heaven can boast.

Amen.

Date: _____

Hymn: *Rejoice, the Lord is King* (all verses)

Rejoice, the Lord is King!
Your Lord and King adore!
Rejoice, give thanks and sing,
And triumph evermore:
Lift up your heart, lift up your voice!
Rejoice, again I say, rejoice!

Jesus, the Savior, reigns,
The God of truth and love;
When He had purged our stains,
He took His seat above;
Lift up your heart, lift up your voice!
Rejoice, again I say, rejoice!

His kingdom cannot fail,
He rules o'er earth and heav'n;
The keys of death and hell
Are to our Jesus given;
Lift up your heart, lift up your voice!
Rejoice, again I say, rejoice!

Amen.

Date: _____

Mid-Year Review by Teacher: _____
Year-End Review by Teacher: _____

2nd Grade

Mark 16:2–8 (The resurrection of Christ)

Very early in the morning, on the first day of the week, they came to the tomb when the sun had risen. And they said among themselves, "Who will roll away the stone from the door of the tomb for us?" But when they looked up, they saw that the stone had been rolled away—for it was very large. And entering the tomb, they saw a young man clothed in a long white robe sitting on the right side; and they were alarmed. But he said to them, "Do not be alarmed. You seek Jesus of Nazareth, who was crucified. He is risen! He is not here. See the place where they laid Him. But go, tell His disciples—and Peter—that He is going before you into Galilee; there you will see Him, as He said to you." So they went out quickly and fled from the tomb, for they trembled and were amazed. And they said nothing to anyone, for they were afraid.

Date: _____

Proverbs 3:5–6

Trust in the LORD with all your heart,
And lean not on your own understanding;
In all your ways acknowledge Him,
And He shall direct your paths.

Date: _____

1 John 3:4

Whoever commits sin also commits lawlessness, and sin is lawlessness.

Date: _____

Psalm 100

Make a joyful shout to the LORD, all you lands!
Serve the LORD with gladness;
Come before His presence with singing.
Know that the LORD, He is God;
It is He who has made us, and not we ourselves;
We are His people and the sheep of His pasture.

Enter into His gates with thanksgiving,
And into His courts with praise.
Be thankful to Him, and bless His name.
For the LORD is good;
His mercy is everlasting,
And His truth endures to all generations.

Date: _____

Proverbs 20:11

Even a child is known by his deeds,
By whether he does what is pure and right.

Date: _____

Psalm 119:1–8

Blessed are the undefiled in the way,
Who walk in the law of the LORD!
Blessed are those who keep His testimonies,
Who seek Him with the whole heart!
They also do no iniquity;
They walk in His ways.
You have commanded us
To keep Your precepts diligently.
Oh, that my ways were directed
To keep Your statutes!
Then I would not be ashamed,
When I look into all Your commandments.
I will praise You with uprightness of heart,
When I learn Your righteous judgments.
I will keep Your statutes;
Oh, do not forsake me utterly!

Date: _____

Names of the Twelve Apostles

1. Simon Peter
2. Andrew
3. James (son of Zebedee)
4. John (son of Zebedee)
5. Philip
6. Bartholomew
7. Matthew
8. Thomas
9. James (son of Alphaeus)
10. Simon
11. Thaddaeus (Judas, son of James)
12. Judas Iscariot

Date: _____

The Apostles' Creed

I believe in God the Father Almighty,
Maker of heaven and earth.

And in Jesus Christ, His only begotten Son, our Lord,
Who was conceived by the Holy Spirit,
Born of the Virgin Mary,
Suffered under Pontius Pilate,
Was crucified, dead and buried;
He descended into hell;
The third day He rose again from the dead:
He ascended into heaven,
And sits on the right hand of God the Father Almighty;
From there He shall come to judge the living and the dead.

I believe in the Holy Spirit,
The holy catholic church,
The communion of saints,
The forgiveness of sins,
The resurrection of the body
And the life everlasting.
Amen.

(NOTE: The meaning of "catholic" is not to be confused with the Roman Catholic Church. It means universal.)

Date: _____

Hymn: This is My Father's World

This is my Father's world,
And to my listening ears,
All nature sings,
And round me rings
The music of the spheres.
This is my Father's world,
I rest me in the thought
Of rocks and trees, of skies and seas;
His hand the wonders wrought.

This is my Father's world,
The birds their carols raise;
The morning light, the lily white
Declare their Maker's praise.
This is my Father's world:
He shines in all that's fair;
In the rustling grass I hear Him pass,
He speaks to me everywhere.

This is my Father's world,
O let me ne'er forget
That though the wrong seems oft so strong,
God is the ruler yet.
This is my Father's world,
The battle is not done;
Jesus who died shall be satisfied,
And earth and heaven be one.

Amen.

Date: _____

Mid-Year Review by Teacher: _____
Year-End Review by Teacher: _____

3rd Grade

John 1:1–4

> In the beginning was the Word, and the Word was with God, and the Word was God. He was in the beginning with God. All things were made through Him, and without Him nothing was made that was made. In Him was life, and the life was the light of men.
>
> Date: _____

John 11:25–26

> Jesus said to her, "I am the resurrection and the life. He who believes in Me, though he may die, he shall live. And whoever lives and believes in Me shall never die. Do you believe this?"
>
> Date: _____

Proverbs 14:12

> There is a way that seems right to a man,
> But its end is the way of death.
>
> Date: _____

John 5:24

> "Most assuredly, I say to you, he who hears My word and believes in Him who sent Me has everlasting life, and shall not come into judgment, but has passed from death into life."
>
> Date: _____

Psalm 19

The heavens declare the glory of God;
And the firmament shows His handiwork.
Day unto day utters speech,
And night unto night reveals knowledge.
There is no speech nor language
Where their voice is not heard.
Their line has gone out through all the earth,
And their words to the end of the world.

In them He has set a tabernacle for the sun,
Which is like a bridegroom coming out of his chamber,
And rejoices like a strong man to run its race.
Its rising is from one end of heaven,
And its circuit to the other end;
And there is nothing hidden from its heat.

The law of the LORD is perfect, converting the soul;
The testimony of the LORD is sure, making wise the simple;
The statutes of the LORD are right, rejoicing the heart;
The commandment of the LORD is pure, enlightening the
    eyes;
The fear of the LORD is clean, enduring forever;
The judgments of the LORD are true and righteous altogether.
More to be desired are they than gold,
Yea, than much fine gold;
Sweeter also than honey and the honeycomb.
Moreover by them Your servant is warned,
And in keeping them there is great reward.

Who can understand his errors?
Cleanse me from secret faults.
Keep back Your servant also from presumptuous sins;
Let them not have dominion over me.
Then I shall be blameless,
And I shall be innocent of great transgression.

Let the words of my mouth and the meditation of my heart
Be acceptable in Your sight,
O LORD, my strength and my Redeemer.

Date: _____

John 14:1–6

"Let not your heart be troubled; you believe in God, believe also in Me. In My Father's house are many mansions; if it were not so, I would have told you. I go to prepare a place for you. And if I go and prepare a place for you, I will come again and receive you to Myself; that where I am, there you may be also. And where I go you know, and the way you know." Thomas said to Him, "Lord, we do not know where You are going, and how can we know the way?" Jesus said to him, "I am the way, the truth, and the life. No one comes to the Father except through Me."

Date: _____

Psalm 119:9–24

How can a young man cleanse his way?
By taking heed according to Your word.
With my whole heart I have sought You;
Oh, let me not wander from Your commandments!
Your word I have hidden in my heart,
That I might not sin against You.
Blessed are You, O LORD!
Teach me Your statutes.
With my lips I have declared
All the judgments of Your mouth.
I have rejoiced in the way of Your testimonies,
As much as in all riches.
I will meditate on Your precepts,
And contemplate Your ways.
I will delight myself in Your statutes;
I will not forget Your word.

Deal bountifully with Your servant,
That I may live and keep Your word.
Open my eyes, that I may see
Wondrous things from Your law.
I am a stranger in the earth;
Do not hide Your commandments from me.
My soul breaks with longing
For Your judgments at all times.
You rebuke the proud—the cursed,
Who stray from Your commandments.
Remove from me reproach and contempt,
For I have kept Your testimonies.
Princes also sit and speak against me,
But Your servant meditates on Your statutes.
Your testimonies also are my delight
And my counselors.

Date: _____

Proverbs 12:26

The righteous should choose his friends carefully,
For the way of the wicked leads them astray.

Date: _____

Hymn: *The Lord is My Shepherd*

The Lord is my Shepherd, no want shall I know;
I feed in green pastures, safe-folded I rest;
He leadeth my soul where the still waters flow,
Restores me when wandering, redeems when oppressed.

Thro' the valley and shadow of death though I stray,
Since Thou art my Guardian, no evil I fear;
Thy rod shall defend me, Thy staff be my stay;
No harm can befall with my Comforter near,
No harm can befall with my Comforter near.

In the midst of affliction my table is spread,
With blessings unmeasured my cup runneth o'er;
With perfume and oil Thou anointest my head;
O what shall I ask of Thy providence more?
O what shall I ask of Thy providence more?

Let goodness and mercy, my bountiful God,
Still follow my steps till I meet Thee above;
I seek, by the path which my forefathers trod.
Thro' the land of their sojourn, Thy Kingdom of love,
Thro' the land of their sojourn, Thy Kingdom of love.

Amen.

Date: _____

Mid-Year Review by Teacher: _____
Year-End Review by Teacher: _____

4th Grade

1 John 5:4–5

For whatever is born of God overcomes the world. And this is the victory that has overcome the world—our faith. Who is he who overcomes the world, but he who believes that Jesus is the Son of God?

Date: _____

Matthew 6:19–21

"Do not lay up for yourselves treasures on earth, where moth and rust destroy and where thieves break in and steal; but lay up for yourselves treasures in heaven, where neither moth nor rust destroys and where thieves do not break in and steal. For where your treasure is, there your heart will be also."

Date: _____

Matthew 6:24–26

"No one can serve two masters; for either he will hate the one and love the other, or else he will be loyal to the one and despise the other. You cannot serve God and mammon. Therefore I say to you, do not worry about your life, what you will eat or what you will drink; nor about your body, what you will put on. Is not life more than food and the body more than clothing? Look at the birds of the air, for they neither sow nor reap nor gather into barns; yet your heavenly Father feeds them. Are you not of more value than they?"

Date: _____

Matthew 5:1–12 (The Beatitudes)

And seeing the multitudes, He went up on a mountain, and when He was seated His disciples came to Him. Then He opened His mouth and taught them, saying:

"Blessed are the poor in spirit,
For theirs is the kingdom of heaven.
Blessed are those who mourn,
For they shall be comforted.
Blessed are the meek,
For they shall inherit the earth.
Blessed are those who hunger and thirst for righteousness,
For they shall be filled.
Blessed are the merciful,
For they shall obtain mercy.
Blessed are the pure in heart,
For they shall see God.
Blessed are the peacemakers,
For they shall be called sons of God.
Blessed are those who are persecuted for righteousness'
sake,
For theirs is the kingdom of heaven.

"Blessed are you when they revile and persecute you, and say all kinds of evil against you falsely for My sake. Rejoice and be exceedingly glad, for great is your reward in heaven, for so they persecuted the prophets who were before you.

Date: _____

Psalm 119:25–40

My soul clings to the dust;
Revive me according to Your word.
I have declared my ways, and You answered me;
Teach me Your statutes.
Make me understand the way of Your precepts;
So shall I meditate on Your wonderful works.
My soul melts from heaviness;
Strengthen me according to Your word.
Remove from me the way of lying,
And grant me Your law graciously.
I have chosen the way of truth;
Your judgments I have laid before me.
I cling to Your testimonies;
O LORD, do not put me to shame!
I will run the course of Your commandments,
For You shall enlarge my heart.

Teach me, O LORD, the way of Your statutes,
And I shall keep it to the end.
Give me understanding, and I shall keep Your law;
Indeed, I shall observe it with my whole heart.
Make me walk in the path of Your commandments,
For I delight in it.
Incline my heart to Your testimonies,
And not to covetousness.
Turn away my eyes from looking at worthless things,
And revive me in Your way.
Establish Your word to Your servant,
Who is devoted to fearing You.
Turn away my reproach which I dread,
For Your judgments are good.
Behold, I long for Your precepts;
Revive me in Your righteousness.

Date: _____

John 10:9–10

I am the door. If anyone enters by Me, he will be saved, and will go in and out and find pasture. The thief does not come except to steal, and to kill, and to destroy. I have come that they may have life, and that they may have it more abundantly.

Date: _____

Hymn: Rock of Ages, Cleft for Me

Rock of Ages, cleft for me,
Let me hide myself in Thee;
Let the water and the blood,
From Thy wounded side which flowed,
Be of sin the double cure;
Save from wrath and make me pure.

Could my tears forever flow,
Could my zeal no languor know,
These for sin could not atone;
Thou must save, and Thou alone;
In my hand no price I bring,
Simply to thy cross I cling.

While I draw this fleeting breath,
When mine eyes shall close in death,
When I rise to worlds unknown,
And behold Thee on Thy throne,
Rock of Ages, cleft for me,
Let me hide myself in Thee.

Amen.

Date: _____

The Books of the Bible:

Old Testament

Genesis	2 Chronicles	Daniel
Exodus	Ezra	Hosea
Leviticus	Nehemiah	Joel
Numbers	Esther	Amos
Deuteronomy	Job	Obadiah
Joshua	Psalm	Jonah
Judges	Proverbs	Micah
Ruth	Ecclesiastes	Nahum
1 Samuel	Song of Solomon	Habakkuk
2 Samuel	Isaiah	Zephaniah
1 Kings	Jeremiah	Haggai
2 Kings	Lamentations	Zechariah
1 Chronicles	Ezekiel	Malachi

Date: _____

New Testament

Matthew	Ephesians	Hebrews
Mark	Philippians	James
Luke	Colossians	1 Peter
John	1 Thessalonians	2 Peter
Acts	2 Thessalonians	1 John
Romans	1 Timothy	2 John
1 Corinthians	2 Timothy	3 John
2 Corinthians	Titus	Jude
Galatians	Philemon	Revelation

Date: _____

Mid-Year Review by Teacher: _____
Year-End Review by Teacher: _____

A Catechism for Boys and Girls

1. **Who made you?**
    God made me.
    (Genesis 1:26, 27; 2:7; Ecclesiastes 12:1; Acts 17:24–29)

    Date: _____

2. **What else did God make?**
    God made all things.
    (Genesis 1, esp. vv. 1, 31; Acts 14:15; Romans 11:36; Colossians 1:16)

    Date: _____

3. **Why did God make you and all things?**
    For His own glory.
    (Psalm 19: 1; Jeremiah 9:23, 24; Revelation 4:11; 5:13)

    Date: _____

4. **How can you glorify God?**
    By loving Him and doing what He commands.
    (Ecclesiastes 12:13; Mark 12:29–31; John 15:8–10; 1 Corinthians 10:31)

    Date: _____

5. **Why ought you to glorify God?**
    Because He made me and takes care of me.
    (Romans 11:36; Revelation 4:11; cf. Daniel 5:23)

    Date: _____

6. **Are there more gods than one?**
    There is only one God.
    (Deuteronomy 6:4; Jeremiah 10:10; Mark 12:29; Acts 17:22–31)

    Date: _____

7. **In how many persons does this one God exist?**
In three persons.
(Matthew 3:16, 17; John 5:23; 10:30; 14:9, 10; 15:26; 16:13 –15; 1 John 5:20, 2 John 9; Revelation 1:4, 5)

Date: _____

8. **Who are they?**
The Father, the Son and the Holy Spirit.
(Matthew 28:19; 2 Corinthians 13:14; 1 Peter 1:2; Jude 20, 21)

Date: _____

9. **Who is God?**
God is a Spirit, and does not have a body like men.
(John 4:24; 2 Corinthians 3:17; 1 Timothy 1:17)

Date: _____

10. **Where is God?**
God is everywhere.
(Psalm 139:7 –12; Jeremiah 23:23, 24; Acts 17:27, 28)

Date: _____

11. **Can you see God?**
No. I cannot see God, but He always sees me.
(Exodus 33:20; John 1: 18; 1 Timothy 6:16; Psalm 139, esp. vv. 1–5: Proverbs 5:21; Hebrews 4:12, 13)

Date: _____

12. **Does God know all things?**
Yes. Nothing can be hidden from God.
(1 Chronicles 28:9; 2 Chronicles 16:9; Luke 12:6, 7; Romans 2:16)

Date: _____

13. **Can God do all things?**
Yes. God can do all His holy will.
(Psalm 147:5; Jeremiah 32:17; Daniel 4:34, 35; Ephesians 1: 11)

Date: _____

14. **Where do you learn how to love and obey God?**
In the Bible alone.
(Job 11:7; Psalm 119:104; Isaiah 8:20; Matthew 22:29; 2 Timothy 3:15–17)

Date: _____

15. **Who wrote the Bible?**
Holy men who were taught by the Holy Spirit.
(1 Peter 1:20, 21; Acts 1: 16; 2 Timothy 3:16; 1 Peter 1:10, 11)

Date: _____

16. **Who were our first parents?**
Adam and Eve.
(Genesis 2:18–25; 3:20; 5:1, 2; Acts 17:26; 1 Timothy 2:13)

Date: _____

17. **Of what were our first parents made?**
God made the body of Adam out of the ground, and formed Eve from the body of Adam.
(Genesis 2:7; 21–23; 3:19; Psalm 103:14)

Date: _____

18. **What did God give Adam and Eve besides bodies?**
He gave them souls that could never die.
(1 Corinthians 15:45: Ecclesiastes 12:7; Zechariah 12:1)

Date: _____

19. **Have you a soul as well as a body?**
Yes. I have a soul that can never die.
(Matthew 10:28; Mark 8:34–38; 12:30)

Date: _____

20. **How do you know that you have a soul?**
Because the Bible tells me so.
(Matthew 10:28; Mark 8:34–38; 12:30)

Date: _____

21. **In what condition did God make Adam and Eve?**
He made them holy and happy.
(Genesis 1:26–28; Psalm 8:4–8)

Date: _____

22. **Did Adam and Eve stay holy and happy?**
No. They sinned against God.
(Genesis 3:1–7; Ecclesiastes 7:29; Hosea 6:7 where "men" = Adam)

Date: _____

23. **What is sin?**
Sin is any transgression of the law of God.
(1 John 3:4; Romans 3:20; James 2:9–11)

Date: _____

24. **What is meant by transgression?**
Doing what God forbids.
(1 Samuel 13:8–14; 15:22, 23; Hosea 6:7; Romans 1:21–32)

Date: _____

25. **What was the sin of our first parents?**
Eating the forbidden fruit.
(Genesis 2:16, 17; 3:6)

Date: _____

A Catechism for Boys and Girls

26. **Why did they eat the forbidden fruit?**
Because they did not believe what God had said.
(Genesis 3:1–6; cf. Hebrews 11:6)

Date: _____

27. **Who tempted them to this sin?**
The devil tempted Eve, and she gave the fruit to Adam.
(Genesis 3:1–13; 2 Corinthians 11:3; 1 Timothy 2:13,14; cf. Revelation 12:9)

Date: _____

28. **What happened to our first parents when they had sinned?**
Instead of being holy and happy, they became sinful and miserable.
(Genesis 3:14 –24; 4:1–24; James 1:14, 15)

Date: _____

29. **What effect did the sin of Adam have on all mankind?**
All mankind is born in a state of sin and misery.
(Psalm 51:5; Romans 5:12, 18, 19; 1 Corinthians 15:21, 22; 1 John 5:19)

Date: _____

30. **What do we inherit from Adam as a result of this original sin?**
A sinful nature.
(1 Kings 8:46; Psalm 14:2, 3; 58:3; Ecclesiastes 9:3; Matthew 15:18–20; John 2:24, 25; Romans 8:7)

Date: _____

31. **What does every sin deserve?**
The anger and judgment of God.
(Deuteronomy 27:26; Romans 1:18; 2:2; Galatians 3:10; Ephesians 5:6)

Date: _____

32. **Can anyone go to heaven with this sinful nature?**
No. Our hearts must be changed before we can be fit for heaven.
(Jeremiah 31:33, 34; Ezekiel 36:25–27; John 1:12, 13; 3:1–10; 1 John 5:1, 4, 18)

Date: _____

33. **What is a change of heart called?**
Regeneration.
(Titus 3:5–6)

Date: _____

34. **Who can change a sinner's heart?**
The Holy Spirit alone.
(John 3:3; Romans 8:6–11; 1 Corinthians 2:9–14; 2 Thessalonians 2:13, 14; Titus 3:5–6)

Date: _____

35. **What is righteousness?**
It is God's goodness.
(Exodus 33:19; 34:6; Psalm 33:5; Hosea 3:5; Romans 11:22)

Date: _____

36. **Can anyone be saved by his own righteousness?**
No. No one is good enough for God.
(Proverbs 20:9; Ecclesiastes 7:20; Romans 3:10–23)

Date: _____

37. **What is a covenant?**
An agreement between two or more persons.
(e.g., 1 Samuel 18:3; Matthew 26:14, 15)

Date: _____

38. What is the covenant of grace?
The agreement God made with His elect people to save them from their sins.
(Genesis 17:1–8; Romans 11:27; Hebrews 10:16, 17)

Date: _____

39. What did Christ undertake in the covenant of grace?
To keep the whole law for His people and to suffer the punishment due to their sins.
(Romans 8:3, 4; Galatians 4:4, 5; Hebrews 9:14, 15)

Date: _____

40. Did our Lord Jesus Christ ever sin?
No. He was holy, blameless and undefiled.
(Hebrews 7:26; Luke 23:47; Hebrews 4:15; 1 Peter 2:22; 1 John 3:5)

Date: _____

41. How could the Son of God suffer?
Christ, the Son of God, took flesh and blood, that He might obey and suffer as a man.
(John 1:14; Romans 8:3; Galatians 4:4; Philippians 2:7, 8; Hebrews 2:14, 17; 4:15)

Date: _____

42. What is meant by the atonement?
Christ satisfying divine justice, by His sufferings and death, in the place of sinners.
(Mark 10:45; Acts 13:38, 39; Romans 3:24–26; 5:8, 9; 2 Corinthians 5:19–21; Galatians 3:13; 1 Peter 3:18)

Date: _____

43. **What did God the Father undertake in the covenant of grace?**
To justify, adopt and sanctify those for whom Christ should die.
(Romans 8:29–33; Hebrews 10:9, 10; 1 Corinthians 1:8, 9; Philippians 1:6; 1 Thessalonians 4:3, 7)

Date: _____

44. **What is justification?**
It is God regarding sinners as if they had never sinned and granting them righteousness.
(Zechariah 3:1–5; Romans 3:24–26; 4:5; 8:33; 2 Corinthians 5:21; Hebrews 8:12)

Date: _____

45. **What is sanctification?**
It is God making sinners holy in heart and conduct.
(John 17:17; Ephesians 2:10; 4:22–24; Philippians 2:12–13; 1 Thessalonians 5:23)

Date: _____

46. **For whom did Christ obey and suffer?**
For those whom the Father had given Him.
(Isaiah 53:8; Matthew 1:21; John 10:11, 15, 16, 26–29; 17:9; Hebrews 2:13)

Date: _____

47. **What kind of life did Christ live on earth?**
A life of perfect obedience to the law of God.
(Matthew 5:17; Romans 10:4; 1 Peter 2:21, 22)

Date: _____

A Catechism for Boys and Girls

48. **What kind of death did Christ die?**
The painful and shameful death of the cross.
(Psalm 22; Isaiah 53; the Gospel records)

Date: _____

49. **Who will be saved?**
Only those who repent of sin and believe in Christ.
(Mark 1:15; Luke 13:3,5; Acts 2:37–41; 16:30, 31; 20:21; 26:20)

Date: _____

50. **What is it to repent?**
To be sorry for sin, and to hate and forsake it because it is displeasing to God.
(Luke 19:8–10; Romans 6:1, 2; 2 Corinthians 7:9–11; 1 Thessalonians 1:9, 10)

Date: _____

51. **What is it to believe in Christ?**
To trust in Christ alone for salvation.
(John 14:6; Acts 4:12; 1 Timothy 2:5; 1 John 5:11, 12)

Date: _____

52. **Can you repent and believe in Christ by your own power?**
No. I can do nothing good without God's Holy Spirit.
(John 3:5, 6; 6:44; Romans 8:2, 5, 8–11; 1 Corinthians 2:9–14; Galatians 5:17, 18; Ephesians 2:4–6)

Date: _____

53. **How can you receive the Holy Spirit?**
God has told us that we must pray to Him for the Holy Spirit.
(Luke 11:9–13; John 4:10; 16:24)

Date: _____

54. **How were godly persons saved before the coming of Christ?**
By believing in the Savior to come.
(John 8:56; Galatians 3:8, 9; 1 Corinthians 10:1–4; Hebrews 9:15; 11:13)

Date: _____

55. **How did they show their faith?**
By offering sacrifices on God's altar.
(Exodus 24:3–8; 1 Chronicles 29:20–25; Hebrews 9:19–23; 10:1; 11:28)

Date: _____

56. **What did these sacrifices represent?**
Christ, the Lamb of God, who was to die for sinners.
(Exodus 12:46; cf. John 19:36; Hebrews 9 & 10; John 1:29; 1 Corinthians 5:7; 1 Peter 1:19)

Date: _____

57. **What does Christ do for His people?**
He does the work of a prophet, a priest and a king.
(Matthew 13:57; John 18:37; Hebrews 1:1–3; 5:5–10; Revelation 1:5)

Date: _____

58. **Why is Christ a prophet?**
Because He teaches us the will of God.
(Deuteronomy 18:15, 18; John 1:18; 4:25; 14:23, 24; 1 John 5:20)

Date: _____

59. **Why is Christ a priest?**
Because He died for our sins and prays to God for us.
(Psalm 110:4; 1 Timothy 2:5, 6; Hebrews 4:14–16; 7:24, 25; 1 John 2:1, 2)

Date: _____

60. **Why is Christ a king?**
Because He rules over us and defends us.
(Psalm 2:6–9; Matthew 28:18–20; Ephesians 1:19–23; Colossians 1:13, 18; Revelation 15:3, 4)

Date: _____

61. **Why do you need Christ as a prophet?**
Because I am ignorant.
(Job 11:7; Matthew 11:25–27; John 6:67, 69; 17:25, 26; 1 Corinthians 2:14–16; 2 Corinthians 4:3–6)

Date: _____

62. **Why do you need Christ as a priest?**
Because I am guilty.
(Proverbs 20:9; Ecclesiastes 7:20; Romans 3:19–23; Hebrews 10:14, 27, 28; 1 John 1:8, 9)

Date: _____

63. **Why do you need Christ as a king?**
Because I am weak and helpless.
(John 15:4, 5; 2 Corinthians 12:9; Philippians 4:13; Colossians 1:11; Jude 24, 25)

Date: _____

64. **How many commandments did God give on Mount Sinai?**
Ten Commandments.
(Exodus 20:1–17; Deuteronomy 5:1–22)

Date: _____

65. **What are the Ten Commandments sometimes called?**
God's moral law.
(Luke 20:25–28; Romans 2:14,15; 10:5)

Date: _____

66. **What do the first four commandments teach?**
Our duty to God.
(Deuteronomy 6:5, 6; 10:12, 13)

Date: _____

67. **What do the last six commandments teach?**
Our duty to our fellow men.
(Deuteronomy 10:19; Micah 6:8; cf. Galatians 6:10)

Date: _____

68. **What is the sum of the Ten Commandments?**
To love God with all my heart, and my neighbor as myself.
(Deuteronomy 6:1–15; 11:1; Matthew 22:35–40; James 2:8)

Date: _____

69. **Who is your neighbor?**
All my fellow men are my neighbors.
(Luke 10:25–37; 6:35)

Date: _____

70. **Is God pleased with those who love and obey Him?**
Yes. He says, "I love them that love Me."
(Proverbs 8:17; Exodus 20:6)

Date: _____

71. **Is God pleased with those who do not love and obey Him?**
No. "God is angry with the wicked every day."
(Psalm 7:11; Malachi 2:17; Proverbs 6:16–19)

Date: _____

72. **What is the first commandment?**
The first commandment is, "You shall have no other gods before Me."
(Exodus 20:3; Deuteronomy 5:7)

Date: _____

73. **What does the first commandment teach us?**
To worship God only.
(Isaiah 45:5, 6; Matthew 4:10; Revelation 22:8, 9)

Date: _____

74. **What is the second commandment?**
The second commandment is, "You shall not make for yourself any carved image, or any likeness of anything that is in heaven above, or that is in the earth beneath, or that is in the water under the earth: you shall not bow down to them nor serve them. For I, the LORD your God, am a jealous God, visiting the iniquity of the fathers on the children to the third and fourth generations of those that hate Me, but showing mercy to thousands, to those who love Me, and keep My commandments."
(Exodus 20:4–6; Deuteronomy 5:8–10)

Date: _____

75. **What does the second commandment teach us?**
To worship God in the right way and to avoid idolatry.
(Isaiah 44:9–20; 46:5–9; John 4:23, 24; Acts 17:29)

Date: _____

76. **What is the third commandment?**
The third commandment is, "You shall not take the name of the LORD your God in vain; for the LORD will not hold him guiltless who takes His name in vain."
(Exodus 20:7; Deuteronomy 5:11)

Date: _____

77. **What does the third commandment teach us?**
To reverence God's name, word and works.
(Isaiah 8:13; Psalm 29:2; 138:2; Revelation 15:3, 4)

Date: _____

78. **What is the fourth commandment?**
The fourth commandment is, "Remember the Sabbath day to keep it holy. Six days you shall labor and do all your work, but the seventh day is the Sabbath of the LORD your God. In it you shall do no work: you nor your son, nor your daughter, nor your manservant, nor your maidservant, nor your cattle, nor your stranger who is within your gates. For in six days the LORD made heaven and earth, the sea, and all that is in them, and rested the seventh day. Therefore the LORD blessed the Sabbath day, and hallowed it."
(Exodus 20:8–11; 23:12; Deuteronomy 5:12–15)

Date: _____

79. **What does the fourth commandment teach us?**
To keep the Sabbath holy.
(Leviticus 19:20; 23:3; Isaiah 58:13, 14)

Date: _____

80. **What day of the week is the Christian Sabbath?**
The first day of the week, called the Lord's Day.
(Acts 20:7; Revelation 1:10)

Date: _____

81. **Why is it called the Lord's Day?**
Because on that day Christ rose from the dead.
(Matthew 28:1; Mark 16:9; Luke 24:1–6; John 20:1)

Date: _____

82. **How should the Sabbath be kept?**
In prayer and praise, in hearing and reading God's Word,
and in doing good to our fellow men.
(Isaiah 58:13, 14; Matthew 12:10–13; Luke 4:16; Acts 20:7;
1 Corinthians 16:2)

Date: _____

83. **What is the fifth commandment?**
The fifth commandment is, "Honor your father and your
mother, that your days may be long upon the land which
the LORD your God is giving you."
(Exodus 20:12; Deuteronomy 5:16)

Date: _____

84. **What does the fifth commandment teach us?**
To love and obey our parents.
(Matthew 15:3–6; Ephesians 6:1–3; Colossians 3:20)

Date: _____

85. **What is the sixth commandment?**
The sixth commandment is, "You shall not murder."
(Exodus 20:13; Deuteronomy 5:17)

Date: _____

86. **What does the sixth commandment teach us?**
To avoid hatred.
(Matthew 5:21–24; 1 John 3:15)

Date: _____

87. **What is the seventh commandment?**
The seventh commandment is, "You shall not commit adultery."
(Exodus 20:14; Deuteronomy 5:18)

Date: _____

88. **What does the seventh commandment teach us?**
To be pure in heart, language and conduct.
(Matthew 5:27, 28; Ephesians 5:3–5; Philippians 4:8, 9)

Date: _____

89. **What is the eighth commandment?**
The eighth commandment is, "You shall not steal."
(Exodus 20:15; Deuteronomy 5:19)

Date: _____

90. **What does the eighth commandment teach us?**
To be honest and not to take the things of others.
(Exodus 23:4; Proverbs 21:6, 7; Ephesians 4:28)

Date: _____

91. **What is the ninth commandment?**
The ninth commandment is, "You shall not bear false witness against your neighbor."
(Exodus 20:16; Deuteronomy 5:20)

Date: _____

92. **What does the ninth commandment teach us?**
To tell the truth and not to speak evil of others.
(Psalm 15:13; Zechariah 8:16; 1 Corinthians 13:6; James 4:11)

Date: _____

93. **What is the tenth commandment?**
The tenth commandment is, "You shall not covet your neighbor's house, you shall not covet your neighbor's wife, nor his manservant, nor his maidservant, nor his ox, nor his donkey, nor any thing that is your neighbor's."
(Exodus 20:17; Deuteronomy 5:21; Romans 7:7)

Date: _____

94. **What does the tenth commandment teach us?**
To be content with what we have.
(Philippians 4:1 1; 1 Timothy 6:6–8; Hebrews 13:5)

Date: _____

95. **Can any man keep these Ten Commandments perfectly?**
No mere man, since the fall of Adam, ever did or can keep the Ten Commandments perfectly.
(Proverbs 20:9; Ecclesiastes 7:20; Romans 3:19, 20; James 2:10; 1 John 1:8, 10)

Date: _____

96. Of what use are the Ten Commandments to us?
They teach us our duty and show us our need of a Savior.
(I Timothy 1:8–11; Romans 3:20; Galatians 3:24)

Date: _____

97. What is prayer?
Prayer is talking with God.
(Genesis 17:22; 18:33; Nehemiah 1:4–11; 2:4; Matthew 6:6; Romans 8:26, 27)

Date: _____

98. In whose name should we pray?
Only in the name of Christ.
(John 14:13, 14; 16:23, 24; Hebrews 4:14–16)

Date: _____

99. What has Christ given to teach us how to pray?
The Lord's Prayer.
(Matthew 6:5–15; Luke 11:1–13)

Date: _____

100. Repeat the Lord's Prayer.
"Our Father in heaven, hallowed be Your name. Your kingdom come. Your will be done on earth, as it is in heaven. Give us this day our daily bread. And forgive us our debts as we forgive our debtors. And do not lead us into temptation, but deliver us from the evil one. For Yours is the kingdom and the power and the glory forever. Amen."

Date: _____

101. **How many petitions are there in the Lord's Prayer?**
Six.

Date: _____

102. **What is the first petition?**
"Hallowed be Your name."
(Matthew 6:9; Luke 11:2)

Date: _____

103. **What do we pray for in the first petition?**
That God's name may be honored by us and all men.
(Psalm 8:1; 72:17–19; 113:1–3; 145:21; Isaiah 8:13)

Date: _____

104. **What is the second petition?**
"Thy kingdom come."
(Matthew 6:10; Luke 11:2)

Date: _____

105. **What do we pray for in the second petition?**
That the gospel may be preached in all the world, and believed and obeyed by us and all men.
(Matthew 28:19, 20; John 17:20, 21; Acts 8:12; 28:30, 31; 2 Thessalonians 3:1)

Date: _____

106. **What is the third petition?**
"Your will be done on earth as it is in heaven."
(Matthew 6:10; Luke 11:2)

Date: _____

107. What do we pray for in the third petition?

That men on earth may serve God as the angels do in heaven.

(Psalm 67; 103:19–22; John 9:31; Revelation 4:11)

Date: _____

108. What is the fourth petition?

"Give us this day our daily bread."

(Matthew 6:11; Luke 11:3)

Date: _____

109. What do we pray for in the fourth petition?

That God will give us all things needful for our bodies.

(Psalm 145:15, 16; Proverbs 30:8, 9; 1 Timothy 4:4, 5)

Date: _____

110. What is the fifth petition?

"And forgive us our debts, as we forgive our debtors."

(Matthew 6:12; Luke 11:4)

Date: _____

111. What do we pray for in the fifth petition?

That God will pardon our sins and help us to forgive those who have sinned against us.

(Psalm 51: Matthew 5:23, 24; 18:21–35; 1 John 4:20, 21)

Date: _____

112. What is the sixth petition?

"And do not lead us into temptation, but deliver us from the evil one."

(Matthew 6:13; Luke 11:4)

Date: _____

113. **What do we pray for in the sixth petition?**
That God will keep us from sin.
(1 Chronicles 4:10; Psalm 119:11; Matthew 26:41)

Date: _____

114. **How does the Holy Spirit bring us to salvation?**
He uses the Bible, which is the Word of God.
(1 Thessalonians 1:5, 6; 2:13; 2 Timothy 3:15, 16; James 1:18; 1 Peter 1:22, 23)

Date: _____

115. **How can we know the Word of God?**
We are commanded to hear, read and search the Scriptures.
(Matthew 21:42; 22:29; 2 Timothy 3:14–17; 1 Peter 2:2; Revelation 3:22)

Date: _____

116. **What is a church?**
An assembly of baptized believers met together under the preaching of the Word of God.
(Matthew 18:20; Acts 2:42)

Date: _____

117. **What two ordinances did Christ give to His Church?**
Baptism and the Lord's Supper.
(Matthew 28:19; 1 Corinthians 11:24–26)

Date: _____

118. Why did Christ give these ordinances?

To show that His disciples belong to Him, and to remind them of what He has done for them.

(Matthew 28:19; 1 Corinthians 11:24–26)

Date: _____

119. What is baptism?

The dipping of believers into water, as a sign of their union with Christ in His death, burial and resurrection.

(John 3:23; Acts 2:41; 8:12, 35–38; Colossians 2:12)

Date: _____

120. What is the purpose of baptism?

To show believers that God has cleansed them from their sins through Jesus Christ.

(Acts 22:16; Colossians 2:11–14)

Date: _____

121. Who are to be baptized?

Only those who repent of their sins and believe in Christ for salvation.

(Acts 2:37–41; 8:12; 18:8; 19:4, 5)

Date: _____

122. Should babies be baptized?

No; because the Bible neither commands it, nor gives any example of it.

Date: _____

123. What is the Lord's Supper?
The eating of bread and the drinking of wine to remember the sufferings and death of Christ.
(Mark 14:22, 24; 1 Corinthians 11:23–29)

Date: _____

124. What does the bread represent?
The body of Christ, broken for our sins.
(Matthew 26:26; 1 Corinthians 11:24)

Date: _____

125. What does the wine represent?
The blood of Christ, shed for our salvation.
(Matthew 26:27, 28; 1 Corinthians 11:25)

Date: _____

126. Who should partake of the Lord's Supper?
Only those who repent of their sins, believe in Christ for salvation and love their fellow men.
(Matthew 5:21–24; 1 Corinthians 10:16, 17; 11:18, 20, 27–33; 1 John 3:24–27; 4:9–11)

Date: _____

127. Did Christ remain in the tomb after His crucifixion?
No. He rose from the tomb on the third day after His death.
(Luke 24:45–47; 1 Corinthians 15:3, 4)

Date: _____

128. Where is Christ now?

In heaven, seated at the right hand of God the Father.

(Romans 8:34; Hebrews 1:3; 10:12; 12:2)

Date: _____

129. Will Christ come again?

Yes. At the last day He will come again to judge the world.

(Matthew 25:31–46; 2 Thessalonians 1:7–10; 2 Timothy 4:1)

Date: _____

130. What happens to men when they die?

The body returns to dust and the soul goes into the world of spirits.

(Genesis 3:19; Ecclesiastes 12:7; 2 Corinthians 5:1–6)

Date: _____

131. Will the bodies of the dead be raised to life again?

Yes. "There will be a resurrection of the dead, both of the just and unjust."

(Daniel 12:2; John 5:28, 29; Acts 24:14, 15)

Date: _____

132. What will happen to the wicked in the day of judgment?

They shall be cast into hell.

(Psalm 9:16, 17; Luke 12:5; Revelation 20:12–15)

Date: _____

133. What is hell?

A place of dreadful and endless punishment.

(Matthew 25:46; Mark 9:43–48; Luke 16:19–31)

Date: _____

134. What will happen to the righteous in the day of judgment?

They shall live with Christ for ever, in a new heaven and new earth.

(Isaiah 66:22; 1 Thessalonians 4;16, 17; 2 Peter 3:10–13; Revelation 21:1–4)

Date: _____

135. What is heaven?

A glorious and happy place, where the righteous shall be forever with the Lord.

(John 14:2, 3; 1 Thessalonians 4:17; Revelation 21:1–4)

Date: _____

CPSIA information can be obtained at www.ICGtesting.com
Printed in the USA
LVOW121948200812

295055LV00004B/2/A

9 780970 524805